Prawns

50 fabulous recipes

Your Promise of Success

Welcome to the world of Confident Cooking, created for you in our test kitchen, where recipes are double-tested by our team of home economists to achieve a high standard of success.

PERIPLUS

PRAWN SCHOOL

The sweet flavour, succulent texture and pretty coral colour of prawns are irresistible, and they feature in recipes from coastal communities around the world, from Asia to the Mediterranean. Once you know the basics of choosing and preparing prawns, you can start enjoying them.

One of the reasons for the popularity of prawns is that they are very simple to prepare and cook. Read on for the few essentials you will need to know about cooking with prawns. Once you've covered the basics you can launch into the recipes.

TYPE AND SIZE
There are many different types of prawns, but seafood sellers often classify them on the basis of their size rather than their species.

Among the many types of prawns, king prawns are one of the most commonly available and widely recognised species. We have used king prawns in all of our recipes except those needing the tiny school prawn. The three sizes we have used are medium king prawns (about 18 cm), large king prawns

THE 1-2-3 GUIDE TO PREPARING PRAWNS

1 Using your fingers, pull the head away from the body, then pull off the legs and peel the shell away from the body. If the prawns are to be served whole, they generally look better with the tails intact, otherwise they can be removed, if preferred.

Try to remove even the tiniest bits of shell so that you don't crunch on them when eating.
2 To remove the intestinal vein from prawns, start at the head end and use a skewer or a small, finely pointed knife to remove the dark vein.

3 To butterfly prawns, slice them down the back without cutting right through, then open the prawn out. To make cutlets, place the prawn between pieces of plastic wrap or greaseproof paper and flatten gently with the palm of your hand.

(about 20 cm) and the extra large, jumbo king prawns (about 24 cm). However, it is fine to substitute other prawn types (e.g. banana, tiger, royal red) as long as you choose prawns that are the same size specified in the recipe.

CHOOSE FRESH

As with all seafood, freshness is paramount. When buying raw prawns, avoid limp and soft ones that smell of ammonia or have any black spots or juices around the shell and head, as they are signs of deterioration. Instead, choose prawns that are fully intact, firm and crisp, with bright shells and a fresh sea scent.

It is best to buy prawns on the day you need them (particularly cooked ones) because they deteriorate rapidly. If that isn't possible, raw prawns should keep for 1–2 days in a covered container in the coldest part of the fridge. Otherwise, you can freeze them by placing unpeeled prawns in a plastic container and covering with water, to form a large ice block. This prevents freezer burn and insulates the prawns. They can be frozen for up to 3 months. To defrost, place the container on a high-rimmed plate on the bottom shelf of the refrigerator overnight and use as soon as they are thawed, draining well before cooking. Use this same method for defrosting bought frozen prawns.

Prawns are usually sold intact, but many fishmongers also sell them peeled. However, peeled prawns are often much more expensive than unpeeled ones, and as you can see on the facing page, they are easy to prepare yourself and have a greater guarantee of freshness.

COOKING WITH PRAWNS

Raw prawns suit most cooking methods, including barbecuing, grilling, pan-frying, stir-frying, deep-frying, poaching, steaming and baking.

When cooking prawns, it is important not to cook them for too long or they will toughen and spoil. When prawns are cooked through, they should have turned pink and be curled.

While ready-cooked prawns are convenient and excellent for salads, they can toughen on re-cooking. They are best reheated as gently and quickly as possible and served immediately.

PRAWN STOCK

When cooking with raw prawns, don't throw away the heads and shells; keep them in the freezer until you have time to make a delicious prawn stock. The heads and shells of 1 kg of raw prawns will make 1 litre of stock.

Start by breaking up the heads and shells slightly, as this releases their flavour, then heat 2 tablespoons of oil in a saucepan, and stir the prawns over medium heat for 10 minutes, or until orange. Pour in 1 litre of water, bring to the boil, then reduce the heat and simmer for 15 minutes. Strain the stock through a fine sieve, discarding the shells. Refrigerate for up to 3 days or freeze for up to 3 months. Bring to the boil before using.

This stock is a good base for making authentic Tom Yum Goong or an enriching bisque. Depending on how the stock will be used, other complementary flavours can be added such as white wine, finely chopped herbs, carrots, celery, ginger, onion or fennel.

TIP: To avoid a smelly garbage bin, keep any prawn shells in the freezer until garbage collection day.

PRAWNS

Add them to pastas and salads for a quick bite, use them in flavoursome soups, let them shine as fingerfood or just serve stir-fried on a bed of rice to enjoy their succulent, tender flesh.

CAJUN PRAWNS WITH SALSA

Prep time: 30 minutes
Cooking time: 10 minutes
Serves 4 (main) or 6 (entrée)

Cajun spice mix
1 tablespoon garlic powder
1 tablespoon onion powder
2 teaspoons dried thyme
2 teaspoons ground white
    pepper
11/2 teaspoons cayenne
    pepper
1/2 teaspoon dried oregano

Tomato salsa
4 Roma tomatoes, seeded
    and chopped
1 large Lebanese cucumber,
    peeled, seeded, chopped
2 tablespoons finely diced
    red onion
2 tablespoons chopped
    fresh coriander
1 tablespoon chopped fresh
    flat-leaf parsley
1 clove garlic, crushed
2 tablespoons olive oil
1 tablespoon lime juice

1.2 kg raw large prawns
100 g butter, melted
2 cups (60 g) watercress,
    washed and picked over
4 spring onions, chopped
lemon wedges, to serve

1 Combine all the spice mix ingredients with 2 teaspoons cracked black pepper.
2 Combine the tomato, cucumber, onion, coriander and parsley in a bowl. Mix the garlic, oil and lime juice together and season well. Add to the bowl and toss together.
3 Peel and devein the prawns, keeping the tails intact. Brush the prawns with the butter and sprinkle generously with the spice mix. Cook on a barbecue hotplate or under a hot grill, turning once, for 2–3 minutes each side, or until a crust forms and the prawns are pink and cooked.
4 Lay some watercress on serving plates, then spoon the salsa over the leaves. Arrange the prawns on top and sprinkle with some chopped spring onion. Serve with lemon wedges on the side.

Nutrition per serve (6): Fat 19 g; Protein 22 g; Carbohydrate 4.5 g; Dietary Fibre 2 g; Cholesterol 187.5 mg; 1095 kJ (260 Cal)

Cajun prawns with salsa

CHERMOULA PRAWNS

Prep time: 25 minutes +
  30 minutes standing
Cooking time: 10 minutes
Serves 4

Chermoula
1/3 cup (80 ml) virgin olive oil
3 tablespoons chopped
  fresh coriander leaves
2 tablespoons chopped
  fresh flat-leaf parsley
2 tablespoons chopped
  preserved lemon rind
2 tablespoons lemon juice
2 cloves garlic, chopped
1 small fresh red chilli,
  seeded and finely chopped
1 teaspoon ground cumin
1/2 teaspoon paprika

20 raw medium prawns
2 cups (370 g) instant
  couscous
11/2 cups (375 ml) boiling
  chicken stock
1 tablespoon olive oil
2 tablespoons shredded
  fresh mint

1 In a food processor, process the chermoula ingredients to a coarse purée, then season to taste with salt.
2 Peel and devein the prawns, keeping the tails intact. Thread a cocktail stick through the body of each prawn to keep them straight, then place them in a non-metallic dish and spoon on the chermoula, turning to coat. Refrigerate, covered, for 30 minutes, turning occasionally.
3 Place the couscous in a heatproof bowl, pour on the boiling stock and oil, cover and leave for 3–4 minutes. Fluff the couscous with a fork and stir in the mint.
4 Arrange the prawns on a foil-lined grill tray and cook under a hot grill for 2–3 minutes each side, or until pink and cooked. Divide the couscous and prawns among four plates.

Nutrition per serve: Fat 25 g; Protein 32 g; Carbohydrate 73 g; Dietary Fibre 2 g; Cholesterol 131 mg; 2700 kJ (645 Cal)

PASTA WITH SEARED PRAWNS

Prep time: 20 minutes
Cooking time: 10 minutes
Serves 2 (main) or 4 (entrée)

8 raw jumbo prawns
2 tablespoons olive oil
100 g unsalted butter,
  chopped
11/2 tablespoons drained
  baby capers
250 g angel hair pasta
1/4 cup (60 ml) lemon juice
1 teaspoon grated lemon rind
1–2 small fresh red chillies,
  seeded and thinly sliced
1/2 cup (15 g) chopped fresh
  flat-leaf parsley
lemon wedges, to serve

1 Remove the heads from the prawns. Slice them down the back without cutting right through, then open them out, leaving the tails and shells intact. Rinse under cold water and pull out the vein. Pat dry, then season lightly.
2 Heat the oil and half the butter in a large frying pan, add the capers and cook for 1 minute. Remove from the pan and set aside. Add the prawns and cook, cut-side-down first, for 2–3 minutes each side, or until pink and cooked. Remove and keep warm.
3 Meanwhile, cook the pasta in a large saucepan of boiling water until *al dente*. Drain, reserving 1–2 tablespoons of the cooking liquid.
4 Melt the remaining butter in the frying pan, add the lemon juice and rind, capers and chilli and stir until fragrant. Add the pasta and parsley and toss until the pasta is coated with the butter. If needed, add some of the reserved cooking liquid to moisten the pasta. Season.
5 Divide the pasta among serving bowls, top with the prawns and serve with a couple of lemon wedges.

Nutrition per serve (4): Fat 31 g; Protein 15 g; Carbohydrate 44 g; Dietary Fibre 2.5 g; Cholesterol 119.5 mg; 2145 kJ (510 Cal)

Chermoula prawns (top), and Pasta with seared prawns

THAI PRAWN CAKES

Prep time: 20 minutes +
  1 hour refrigeration
Cooking time: 15 minutes
Makes 20

Dipping sauce
1 small Lebanese cucumber,
  finely chopped
1/4 cup (60 ml) sweet chilli
  sauce
2 tablespoons rice vinegar
1 tablespoon chopped
  unsalted peanuts

450 g raw prawn meat,
  deveined
2 spring onions, finely
  chopped
2 tablespoons good-quality
  ready-made red curry paste
2 tablespoons chopped
  fresh coriander leaves
1 tablespoon lime juice
1 teaspoon finely chopped
  fresh green chilli
1 fresh kaffir lime leaf, finely
  chopped
2 tablespoons vegetable oil

1 To make the dipping
sauce, combine all the
ingredients in a bowl.
2 Put the prawn meat,
spring onion, curry
paste, coriander, lime
juice, chilli and kaffir
lime leaf in a food
processor and pulse until
finely minced, but not
as fine as a paste.
3 Take 1 tablespoon
of the mixture at a time
and use your hands to
form into cakes. Place
the cakes on a floured

baking tray in the
refrigerator for 1 hour.
4 Heat the oil in a
frying pan and cook the
prawn cakes in batches
over medium–high heat
for about 1–2 minutes
each side, or until lightly
golden and cooked
through. Serve with
the dipping sauce.

Nutrition per cake: Fat 3 g;
Protein 5 g; Carbohydrate 1 g;
Dietary Fibre 0.5 g; Cholesterol
33.5 mg; 210 kJ (50 Cal)

PRAWN
SUSHI CONES

Prep time: 30 minutes +
  1 hour 10 minutes standing
Cooking time: 20 minutes
Makes 16

11/2 cups (330 g) sushi rice
  or short-grain rice
2 tablespoons seasoned rice
  vinegar
1 avocado
1 small Lebanese cucumber
8 sheets nori, cut in half on
  the diagonal
1 teaspoon wasabi paste
80 g pickled ginger
16 cooked medium prawns,
  peeled and deveined
soy sauce, to serve

1 Place the rice in a
sieve and rinse under
cold running water. Set
aside to drain for 1 hour.
Place the drained rice in
a large saucepan and add
11/2 cups (375 ml) water.

Cover and bring to the
boil, then reduce the
heat to very low and
cook, tightly covered,
for 15 minutes. Remove
from the heat and leave
the lid on for 10 minutes.
2 Transfer the rice to a
large shallow bowl and
drizzle with the vinegar.
Fold the vinegar through
the rice, tossing lightly
with a large metal spoon
or spatula to cool as you
combine. Do not use a
stirring action; it will
make the rice mushy.
3 Quarter and peel the
avocado and cut each
quarter into four long
wedges. Trim the ends of
the cucumber, then cut
lengthways into 16 strips.
4 Hold a sheet of nori
shiny-side-down, flat in
your hand. Place
2 tablespoons of rice on
the left-hand side and
spread out over half the
nori sheet. Dab with a
little wasabi and top with
some pickled ginger.
Place a strip each of
avocado and cucumber
on the rice and top with
one prawn. Roll up the
nori to form a cone,
enclosing the smaller
end. Repeat, using all
the ingredients. Serve
with soy sauce.

Nutrition per cone: Fat 3.5 g;
Protein 3 g; Carbohydrate 17.5 g;
Dietary Fibre 1 g; Cholesterol
11.5 mg; 485 kJ (115 Cal)

Thai prawn cakes (top), and
Prawn sushi cones

PRAWNS WITH SAFFRON POTATOES

Prep time: 15 minutes
Cooking time: 30 minutes
Serves 4

16 raw medium prawns
1/3 cup (80 ml) olive oil
450 g new potatoes, cut
  in half
1/4 teaspoon saffron
  threads, crushed
1 clove garlic, crushed
1 bird's eye chilli, seeded
  and finely chopped
1 teaspoon grated lime rind
1/4 cup (60 ml) lime juice
200 g baby rocket

1 Preheat the oven to moderate 180°C (350°F/Gas 4). Peel and devein the prawns, leaving the tails intact.
2 Heat 2 tablespoons of the oil in a frying pan and brown the potatoes. Transfer to a roasting tin and toss gently with the saffron and some salt and black pepper. Bake for 25 minutes, or until tender.
3 Heat a chargrill pan over medium heat. Toss the prawns with the garlic, chilli, lime rind and 1 tablespoon of the oil in a small bowl. Grill the prawns for 2 minutes each side,

Prawns with saffron potatoes (top), and Tandoori prawn pizza

or until pink and cooked.
4 In a small jar, shake up the lime juice and the remaining oil. Season with salt and pepper. Place the potatoes on a plate, top with the rocket and prawns and drizzle with dressing.

Nutrition per serve: Fat 12.5 g; Protein 19 g; Carbohydrate 17 g; Dietary Fibre 3.5 g; Cholesterol 106 mg; 1065 kJ (255 Cal)

TANDOORI PRAWN PIZZA

Prep time: 20 minutes
Cooking time: 25 minutes
Serves 4

Raita
1 small Lebanese cucumber
11/3 cups (340 g) plain
  yoghurt
1 small clove garlic, crushed
1/2 teaspoon ground cumin
pinch of cayenne pepper

1 tablespoon olive oil
2 teaspoons ground paprika
1/2 teaspoon ground cumin
1/4 teaspoon ground
  cardamom
1/4 teaspoon ground ginger
1/4 teaspoon cayenne
  pepper
1/3 cup (90 g) plain yoghurt
1 teaspoon lemon juice
2 cloves garlic, crushed
16 raw medium prawns,
  peeled and deveined, with
  tails intact
30 cm (300 g) ready-made
  pizza base

1 onion, halved and sliced
1 small red capsicum,
  halved and sliced
3 tablespoons torn fresh
  basil

1 To make the raita, peel the cucumber, scrape out the seeds and coarsely grate the flesh into a bowl with the other ingredients. Stir everything together, then refrigerate.
2 Preheat the oven to hot 220°C (425°F/Gas 7). Heat the oil in a frying pan over medium heat, add the spices and cook until the oil starts to bubble, then cook for another minute. Stir in the yoghurt, lemon juice and garlic, then add the prawns. Cook for 5 minutes, or until the prawns are pink and cooked.
3 Remove the prawns from the tandoori sauce with a slotted spoon and spread the sauce over the pizza base, leaving a 1 cm border. Sprinkle with some of the onion and capsicum, then arrange all the prawns on top. Top with the remaining onion and capsicum and bake for about 15–20 minutes. Scatter with basil, then serve with the raita.

Nutrition per serve: Fat 10.5 g; Protein 29 g; Carbohydrate 51 g; Dietary Fibre 4.5 g; Cholesterol 120 mg; 1740 kJ (415 Cal)

CHU CHEE PRAWN CURRY

Prep time: 30 minutes +
  10 minutes soaking
Cooking time: 20 minutes
Serves 4

10 large dried red chillies
1 kg raw medium prawns
2 teaspoons coriander seeds
1 teaspoon white
  peppercorns
2 teaspoons shrimp paste
2 tablespoons chopped
  fresh coriander roots
1 stem lemon grass (white
  part only), coarsely
  chopped
2 tablespoons fresh
  galangal, peeled and finely
  chopped (see Notes)
6 cloves garlic, chopped
10 red Asian shallots,
  chopped (see Notes)
14 fresh kaffir lime leaves,
  shredded
400 ml can coconut cream
  (do not shake the can)
2–3 tablespoons fish sauce
2 tablespoons grated palm
  sugar or soft brown sugar
1 fresh red chilli, finely
  chopped
20 g fresh Thai basil (see
  Notes)

1 Place the chillies in a bowl and cover with hot water for 10 minutes. Drain the chillies, remove the seeds, then chop and put in a food processor.
2 Peel and devein the prawns, keeping the tails intact. Place the coriander seeds and white peppercorns in a dry frying pan and cook over medium heat for 1–2 minutes, or until fragrant. Transfer to the food processor.
3 Wrap the shrimp paste in foil, then place under a hot grill and cook for 3 minutes, turning once. Add the paste to the food processor.
4 To make the curry paste, add the coriander roots, lemon grass, galangal, garlic, shallots and eight of the shredded kaffir lime leaves to the food processor and blend until smooth—you may need to add a little water if the mixture is too thick. Set aside until needed. (You will only need to use half the curry paste; the rest can be kept in an airtight jar, covered with a little oil, in the fridge for up to 1 week or frozen for up to 3 months.)
5 Remove 1 cup (250 ml) of the thick coconut cream from the top of the can and place in a wok over medium–high heat until it simmers, then add 1/3 cup (100 g) of the curry paste. Bring to the boil, then reduce the heat and simmer for 8 minutes, or until it starts to look slightly oily and begins to separate.
6 Stir in the prawns so that they are thoroughly coated in the curry, then add the remaining thin coconut cream and cook for 5 minutes. Add the fish sauce, palm sugar, fresh red chilli and the remaining shredded kaffir lime leaves and cook for a further 1–2 minutes.
7 Stir in half the basil leaves and garnish with the remainder. Serve with rice and stir-fried or steamed Asian vegetables.

Nutrition per serve: Fat 22 g; Protein 30 g; Carbohydrate 13 g; Dietary Fibre 4 g; Cholesterol 188 mg; 1535 kJ (365 Cal)

Notes: Galangal is a rhizome that is a member of the ginger family. Despite its similarity to ginger, it has a distinct taste and can't be suitably replaced.

Red Asian shallots are small purplish red onions with a concentrated flavour, often used in Southeast Asian cookery. They grow in bulbs and are sold in segments that look like large cloves of garlic. If necessary, you can substitute one small red onion for 3–4 red Asian shallots.

Thai basil has smaller and darker leaves than regular basil and is extensively used in Southeast Asian cooking. The stems and younger leaves have a purple tinge and the flowers are pink. The flavour is a blend of aniseed and cloves. It is available in Asian food stores. You can replace it with regular basil.

Chu chee prawn curry

PRAWN, TOMATO AND SAFFRON PASTA

Prep time: 20 minutes
Cooking time: 20 minutes
Serves 4–6

400 g tagliatelle
2 tablespoons olive oil
1 onion, diced
3 cloves garlic, chopped
    with 1 teaspoon salt
2 pinches of saffron threads
1 red capsicum, diced
1 kg raw medium prawns,
    peeled and deveined, with
    tails intact
300 ml cream
1/4 cup (60 ml) dry white
    wine
1/4 cup (60 ml) fish or
    chicken stock
5 Roma tomatoes, peeled,
    seeded and diced
1 cup (60 g) roughly
    chopped fresh basil
2 tablespoons chopped
    fresh flat-leaf parsley
40 g Parmesan shavings

1 Cook the pasta in a large saucepan of boiling salted water until *al dente*. Drain and keep warm.
2 Meanwhile, heat the oil in a frying pan, add the onion, garlic, saffron and capsicum and stir over medium heat for 2 minutes before adding the prawns. Cook for 2–3 minutes, or until

pink and cooked. Remove the prawns with tongs and set aside.
3 Add the cream, wine, stock and tomato to the pan and cook for 10 minutes, or until reduced slightly. Add the herbs and the cooked prawns. Season.
4 Toss with the pasta and serve with Parmesan.

Nutrition per serve (6): Fat 31 g; Protein 31 g; Carbohydrate 51 g; Dietary Fibre 3.5 g; Cholesterol 212.5 mg; 2570 kJ (615 Cal)

PRAWN MILLEFEUILLE

Prep time: 40 minutes
Cooking time: 15 minutes
Serves 4

Lemon mayonnaise
1 egg yolk
1/2 teaspoon Dijon mustard
pinch of sugar
1 teaspoon cider vinegar
1 teaspoon finely grated
    lemon rind
1 tablespoon lemon juice
2/3 cup (180 ml) oil

2 sheets ready-rolled frozen
    puff pastry, thawed
750 g cooked medium
    prawns
75 g rocket leaves, torn
1/2 small red onion, thinly
    sliced into rings
2 tablespoons capers,
    drained and rinsed
1 tablespoon chopped fresh
    flat-leaf parsley

1 Preheat the oven to moderately hot 200°C (400°F/Gas 6) and line two baking trays with baking paper. To make the lemon mayonnaise, combine the egg yolk, mustard, sugar, vinegar, lemon rind and juice in a bowl. Gradually add the oil, at first drop by drop, then in a thin steady stream, beating continuously with a whisk or wooden spoon until it thickens. Season.
2 Cut the pastry sheets into quarters, then place well apart on the baking trays. Bake for about 15 minutes, or until golden and puffed. Cool for 2 minutes before lifting with a spatula onto a wire rack to cool.
3 Peel and devein the prawns, then cut them in half lengthways. Using half the rocket leaves, prawns, onion rings and capers, make a neat pile on four serving plates and drizzle with some of the mayonnaise. Place a piece of pastry over the salad, then add the remaining ingredients, including some mayonnaise, to the top of the pastry square. Finish with another piece of pastry, sprinkle with parsley and serve.

Nutrition per serve: Fat 53.5 g; Protein 24 g; Carbohydrate 19 g; Dietary Fibre 1 g; Cholesterol 197 mg; 2700 kJ (645 Cal)

Prawn, tomato and saffron pasta (top), and Prawn millefeuille

PRAWN SALAD WITH ASIAN DRESSING

Prep time: 25 minutes
Cooking time: 5 minutes
Serves 4

Dressing
1/3 cup (80 ml) rice vinegar (see Note)
1/4 cup (60 ml) soy sauce
2 tablespoons honey
1 teaspoon sesame oil
1–2 teaspoons grated fresh ginger
2 cloves garlic, crushed

2 carrots (150 g), cut into thin 5 cm long strips
1 red capsicum, thinly sliced
1/2 daikon radish (75 g), peeled and cut into thin 5 cm long strips
10 g garlic chives, cut into 5 cm lengths
750 g cooked medium prawns, peeled and deveined, with tails intact
200 g baby English spinach leaves

1 Place all the dressing ingredients in a small saucepan and warm over medium heat for 2–3 minutes, or until the honey dissolves; do not boil. Remove the pan from the heat.
2 Place the thin strips of carrot, capsicum, radish and garlic chives in a bowl and toss with tongs to evenly distribute. Add the prawns to the vegetables, pour on half the dressing, then toss thoroughly again.
3 To assemble the salad, make a bed of spinach on four plates (or a platter), place the mixed vegetable strips and prawns on the spinach and drizzle with the remaining dressing. Serve immediately.

Nutrition per serve: Fat 2 g; Protein 22 g; Carbohydrate 15 g; Dietary Fibre 3 g; Cholesterol 139.5 mg; 715 kJ (170 Cal)

Note: Rice vinegar is a pale yellow sweet-tasting vinegar made from rice. There aren't really any suitable substitutes.

INDIAN-STYLE BUTTER PRAWNS

Prep time: 15 minutes
Cooking time: 25 minutes
Serves 4

1 kg raw large prawns
100 g butter
2 large cloves garlic, crushed
1 teaspoon ground cumin
1 teaspoon paprika
1 1/2 teaspoons garam masala
2 tablespoons good-quality ready-made tandoori paste
2 tablespoons tomato paste
300 ml thick cream
1 teaspoon sugar
1/3 cup (90 g) plain yoghurt
2 tablespoons chopped fresh coriander leaves
1 tablespoon flaked almonds, toasted
lemon wedges, to serve

1 Peel and devein the prawns, leaving the tails intact. Melt the butter in a large saucepan over medium heat, then add the garlic, cumin, paprika and 1 teaspoon of the garam masala and cook for 1 minute, or until fragrant. Add the tandoori and tomato pastes and cook for a further 2 minutes. Stir in the cream and sugar, then reduce the heat and simmer for 10 minutes, or until the sauce thickens slightly.
2 Add the prawns to the pan and cook for 8–10 minutes, or until they are pink and cooked through. Remove the pan from the heat and stir in the yoghurt, the remaining garam masala and half the coriander. Season.
3 Garnish with the flaked almonds and remaining coriander and serve with steamed rice and lemon wedges.

Nutrition per serve: Fat 54 g; Protein 30.5 g; Carbohydrate 8 g; Dietary Fibre 2.5 g; Cholesterol 336 mg; 2660 kJ (635 Cal)

Note: This dish is very rich so we recommend that you serve it with steamed green beans or a crispy salad.

Prawn salad with Asian dressing (top), and Indian-style butter prawns

PRAWN TACOS

Prep time: 20 minutes
Cooking time: 20 minutes
Serves 4

2 firm ripe tomatoes, seeded
  and diced
2 tablespoons lime juice
1/2 teaspoon chilli powder
1/2 teaspoon ground cumin
2 tablespoons oil
1 red onion, diced
4 cloves garlic, crushed
18 raw medium prawns,
  peeled, deveined and
  roughly chopped
3 tablespoons chopped
  fresh flat-leaf parsley
8 corn taco shells
150 g shredded iceberg
  lettuce
1 avocado, diced
1/2 cup (125 g) sour cream

1 Preheat the oven to
moderate 180°C (350°F/
Gas 4).
2 Combine the tomato,
lime juice, chilli powder
and cumin in a bowl.
3 Heat the oil in a
frying pan, add the
onion and garlic and
cook for 3–5 minutes,
or until soft. Stir in the
tomato mixture and cook
for 2 minutes. Add the
prawn meat and parsley
and cook for 3–5 minutes,
or until the prawns
are pink and cooked.
Meanwhile, heat the
taco shells on a baking
tray in the oven for
5 minutes.
4 Place some lettuce in
the bottom of each taco
shell, then fill with the
prawn mixture. Top
with some avocado and
a dollop of sour cream,
then serve.

Nutrition per serve: Fat 41.5 g;
Protein 21 g; Carbohydrate 18 g;
Dietary Fibre 5.5 g; Cholesterol
154 mg; 2205 kJ (525 Cal)

TEQUILA-LIME GRILLED PRAWNS

Prep time: 20 minutes +
  1 hour standing
Cooking time: 5 minutes
Serves 4

32 raw large prawns
1/2 cup (125 ml) lime juice
1/4 cup (60 ml) tequila
2 small fresh red chillies,
  finely chopped
3 tablespoons chopped
  fresh coriander leaves
2 tablespoons olive oil
2 cloves garlic, crushed

Green tomato salsa
1 green tomato, seeded and
  diced
2 tablespoons finely
  chopped red onion
2 fresh green chillies, seeded
  and finely diced
1/2 cup (25 g) chopped fresh
  coriander leaves
1 clove garlic, chopped
1 tablespoon olive oil
1 avocado
1 tablespoon lime juice

1 Soak eight wooden
skewers in cold water
for 30 minutes. Peel
and devein the prawns,
leaving the tails intact.
Thread four prawns onto
each skewer. Lay out the
skewers in a single layer
in a non-metallic dish.
2 Combine the lime
juice, tequila, chilli,
coriander, oil and garlic
in a small jug, then pour
over the prawns. Cover
and marinate in the
fridge for 30 minutes.
3 To make the salsa,
mix together the tomato,
onion, chilli, coriander,
garlic and olive oil,
then season. Cover and
refrigerate until needed.
4 Cook the skewers
on a hot lightly oiled
chargrill pan or barbecue
hot plate for 3–5 minutes,
or until pink and cooked
through, brushing with
the marinade during
cooking to keep the
prawns moist.
5 Before serving, halve
the avocado, remove the
stone, cut the flesh into
1 cm dice, then gently
mix the avocado into the
salsa, stirring in the lime
juice at the same time.
Season to taste, then
serve with the prawns.

Nutrition per serve: Fat 25 g;
Protein 34 g; Carbohydrate 8.5 g;
Dietary Fibre 2 g; Cholesterol
226.5 mg; 1750 kJ (420 Cal)

Prawn tacos (top), and
Tequila-lime grilled prawns

PRAWN BISQUE

Prep time: 10 minutes +
refrigeration
Cooking time: 1 hour
Serves 4

120 g unsalted butter
1/2 onion, finely diced
1/2 carrot, finely diced
1/2 celery stick, finely diced
1 clove garlic, finely chopped
750 g raw medium prawns
1 tablespoon brandy
1 tablespoon tomato paste
1 bay leaf
1 tablespoon fresh tarragon,
    finely chopped
pinch of cayenne pepper
200 ml dry white wine
850 ml fish or chicken stock
1/2 cup (125 ml) double thick
    cream
pinch cayenne pepper

1 Heat 25 g of the butter in a saucepan over high heat until it melts. Add the diced vegetables and the garlic, cover and cook over medium–high heat for 5 minutes, or until the vegetables are soft but not coloured. Add the whole prawns and cook for 5 minutes, or until the prawns start to turn pink.

2 Increase the heat to high, pour in the brandy, let it come to the boil then set it alight with a long match. When the flame is out, add the tomato paste, bay leaf, tarragon and cayenne and stir for 4–5 minutes, or until mixed and the tomato paste changes colour and looks a little dry. Cover with the white wine and allow it to evaporate to a syrup, then add 600 ml of the stock. Bring to the boil, reduce the heat, cover and simmer gently for 18–20 minutes. Strain into a bowl, reserving the prawns and liquid separately. Return the liquid to the saucepan.

3 Remove the prawns from the strainer and set six whole prawns aside to make the prawn butter. Peel and devein the remainder of the prawns, reserving the heads and shells. Set aside four peeled prawns for a garnish. Place the remaining peeled prawns in a blender with 1/2 cup (125 ml) of the reserved liquid and all the reserved prawn heads and shells. Pulse until blended but still coarse, then strain into the saucepan with the rest of the reserved liquid. Reserve the prawn remnants in the sieve. Return the soup to simmering point while the butter is being made, occasionally skimming any visible oil from the surface with a spoon.

4 Meanwhile, to make the prawn butter, heat the remaining butter in a small saucepan, add the reserved prawn remnants from the sieve and the reserved six whole prawns, then sauté for 2–3 minutes, stirring until thoroughly heated. Transfer the mixture to a blender to purée, then scrape the purée through a fine sieve, mashing with a wooden spoon to obtain as much butter as possible. Refrigerate the butter mixture and allow to cool and set.

5 Strain the soup through a fine sieve into a clean saucepan to help make the soup smooth and get rid of the excess oil. Reheat the soup gently, then dilute with the remaining 1 cup (250 ml) of the stock, if desired. Just before serving, whisk in the cream.

6 Remove the soup from the heat and stir in the prawn butter a teaspoon at a time until it is all mixed in. Season to taste with another pinch of cayenne, and some salt and pepper. Serve immediately with Melba toast, croutons or fresh bread and garnish with a reserved peeled prawn in each bowl.

Nutrition per serve: Fat 36 g;
Protein 43 g; Carbohydrate 5 g;
Dietary Fibre 1 g; Cholesterol
384.5 mg; 2320 kJ (555 Cal)

Prawn bisque

LEMON GRASS PRAWN STICKS

Prep time: 15 minutes +
   10 minutes freezing
Cooking time: 10 minutes
Makes 8

1 teaspoon grated palm
   sugar or soft brown sugar
1 tablespoon lime juice
1 bird's eye chilli, finely
   chopped
1 small clove garlic, finely
   chopped
2 1/2 tablespoons fish sauce
500 g raw medium prawns,
   peeled and deveined
1 egg white
2 tablespoons roughly
   chopped fresh coriander
   leaves
8 stems lemon grass (white
   part only), trimmed
1/2 cup (125 ml) oil
   (e.g. canola, sunflower,
   safflower or grapeseed)

1 To make the dipping sauce, combine the sugar, lime juice, chilli, garlic and 2 tablespoons of the fish sauce in a small bowl and stir until the sugar dissolves. Set aside until needed.
2 Place the prawns, egg white, remaining fish sauce and a little salt and pepper in a food processor and process to a mince. Add the coriander and pulse briefly. Transfer the mixture to the freezer for 5–10 minutes to ensure easier handling.
3 Divide the mince into eight even portions. Using wet hands, mould one portion of the mince onto the root end of each lemon grass stem.
4 Pour the oil into a frying pan and heat over medium–high, then add the prawn sticks, four at a time. Cook for 2 minutes each side, or until golden and cooked through. Serve with the dipping sauce.

Nutrition per stick: Fat 9.5 g;
Protein 7.5 g; Carbohydrate 1 g;
Dietary Fibre 0.5 g; Cholesterol
46.5 mg; 505 kJ (120 Cal)

VIETNAMESE PRAWN AND CABBAGE SALAD

Prep time: 25 minutes
Cooking time: 10 minutes
Serves 4

1/3 cup (80 ml) rice vinegar
2 tablespoons fish sauce
2 tablespoons lime juice
2 tablespoons grated palm
   sugar or soft brown sugar
1 small fresh red chilli,
   seeded and finely chopped
2 tablespoons peanut oil
1 clove garlic, crushed
20 raw medium prawns,
   peeled and deveined with
   tails intact
2 cups (150 g) thinly sliced
   cabbage
2 cups (150 g) thinly sliced
   red cabbage
200 g sliced drained
   bamboo shoots
1/2 cup (10 g) fresh mint
   leaves
1/2 cup (15 g) fresh
   coriander leaves
2 fresh long green chillies,
   seeded and thinly sliced
   on the diagonal
lime wedges, to serve

1 To make the salad dressing, combine the rice vinegar, fish sauce, lime juice, palm sugar and red chilli in a small bowl and stir together until the sugar has dissolved.
2 Heat the peanut oil in a non-stick frying pan or wok over medium heat. When hot, add the garlic and cook for 10 seconds, stirring constantly. Add the prawns in two batches and cook for about 2 minutes each side, or until pink and cooked through, then remove from the pan.
3 Place the cabbages, bamboo shoots, herbs and green chilli in a serving bowl and mix together. Add the prawns to the bowl, pour the dressing over the salad, season with pepper and toss well. Serve with lime wedges.

Nutrition per serve: Fat 9 g;
Protein 21 g; Carbohydrate 10 g;
Dietary Fibre 4.5 g; Cholesterol
127.5 mg; 860 kJ (205 Cal)

Lemon grass prawn sticks
(top), and Vietnamese prawn
and cabbage salad

PRAWN AND DILL SPAGHETTINI

Prep time: 15 minutes
Cooking time: 20 minutes
Serves 6

500 g spaghettini
100 ml olive oil
2 cloves garlic, crushed
30 raw medium prawns, peeled and deveined
2 tablespoons chopped fresh dill
1 tablespoon chopped fresh flat-leaf parsley
2 tablespoons capers, drained and rinsed
1 tablespoon lemon juice
1/2 cup (75 g) crumbled feta
lemon wedges, to serve

1 Cook the pasta in a large saucepan of boiling water until *al dente*. Drain, then transfer to a large bowl and toss with 1/4 cup (60 ml) of the oil.
2 Meanwhile, heat a non-stick frying pan over medium heat, heat the remaining oil, then add the garlic and cook, stirring, for 30 seconds. Add the prawns and cook for 2 minutes each side, or until pink and cooked. Add to the bowl with the pasta, then add the herbs and capers. Toss well. Pour the lemon juice over the pasta, toss again, then divide among six plates. Sprinkle each plate with a tablespoon of feta and serve with lemon wedges.

Nutrition per serve: Fat 18 g; Protein 30 g; Carbohydrate 58 g; Dietary Fibre 3 g; Cholesterol 140.5 mg; 2095 kJ (500 Cal)

PRAWN RISOTTO

Prep time: 20 minutes
Cooking time:
  1 hour 25 minutes
Serves 4–6

1 kg raw medium prawns
2 tomatoes, chopped
1 carrot, chopped
1 celery stick, chopped
2 bay leaves
1 large onion, chopped
5 cloves garlic, crushed
1 cup (250 ml) dry white wine
pinch of saffron threads
1 tablespoon olive oil
20 g butter
11/2 cups (330 g) arborio rice
1 teaspoon finely grated lemon rind
3 tablespoons finely chopped fresh flat-leaf parsley
1 tablespoon lemon juice
shaved Parmesan, to serve

1 Peel and devein the prawns. Reserve the heads and shells. Cover the prawns, then refrigerate. Place the heads and shells in a large saucepan and add 1.5 litres water. Bring to the boil, then reduce the heat and simmer for 5 minutes.
2 Strain the liquid into a clean saucepan and add the tomato, carrot, celery, bay leaves, half the onion and half the garlic. Bring to the boil, then reduce the heat and simmer for 45 minutes. Strain into a bowl, pressing the solids for any juices, then return the liquid to the same pan—you should have 1.25 litres liquid; if not, add water. Add the wine and saffron, bring to the boil, then reduce the heat and keep at a simmer.
3 Heat the oil and butter in a large saucepan over medium heat until the butter melts, then add the remaining onion and cook for 5 minutes, or until soft. Add the rice and remaining garlic and stir for 1 minute, or until the rice is well coated.
4 Ladle 1/2 cup (125 ml) of the stock into the rice and stir constantly until it is all absorbed. Add stock, 1/2 cup (125 ml) at a time, stirring constantly for 25 minutes, or until all the stock is absorbed, adding the raw prawns and lemon rind with the final portion of stock. When the prawns are pink and curled and the rice is tender and creamy, stir in the parsley and lemon juice. Season and serve with Parmesan.

Nutrition per serve (6): Fat 8 g; Protein 27 g; Carbohydrate 12 g; Dietary Fibre 1.5 g; Cholesterol 186 mg; 990 kJ (235 Cal)

Prawn and dill spaghettini (top), and Prawn risotto

CRUMBED PRAWNS WITH PONZU DIPPING SAUCE

Prep time: 15 minutes
Cooking time: 10 minutes
Makes 18

18 raw jumbo prawns
2 tablespoons cornflour
3 eggs
3 cups (240 g) fresh
 breadcrumbs
oil, for pan-frying
1/3 cup (80 ml) ponzu sauce
 or 1/4 cup (60 ml) soy
 sauce combined with
 1 tablespoon lemon juice

1 Peel and devein the prawns, leaving the tails intact. Cut down the back of each prawn to form a butterfly. Place each prawn between two layers of plastic wrap and gently beat to form a cutlet.
2 Put the cornflour, eggs and breadcrumbs in separate bowls. Lightly beat the eggs. Dip each prawn first into the cornflour then into the egg and finally into the breadcrumbs, ensuring that each cutlet is well covered in crumbs.
3 Heat the oil in a frying pan over medium heat until hot. Cook six prawn cutlets at a time for about 1 minute each side, or until the crumbs are golden—be careful they don't burn. Serve immediately with ponzu sauce.

Nutrition per prawn: Fat 4.5 g; Protein 7 g; Carbohydrate 10 g; Dietary Fibre 0.5 g; Cholesterol 59.5 mg; 453 kJ (108 Cal)

Note: Ponzu sauce is a Japanese dipping sauce usually used for sashimi.

SWEET CHILLI PRAWNS

Prep time: 20 minutes
Cooking time: 10 minutes
Serves 4

1 kg raw medium prawns
2 tablespoons peanut oil
1 cm x 3 cm piece fresh
 ginger, cut into julienne
 strips
2 cloves garlic, finely
 chopped
5 spring onions, cut into
 3 cm lengths
1/3 cup (80 ml) chilli garlic
 sauce
2 tablespoons tomato sauce
2 tablespoons Chinese rice
 wine (see Notes)
1 tablespoon Chinese black
 vinegar or rice vinegar
 (see Notes)
1 tablespoon soy sauce
1 tablespoon soft brown
 sugar
1 teaspoon cornflour mixed
 with 1/2 cup (125 ml) water
finely chopped spring onion,
 to garnish

1 Peel and devein the prawns, leaving the tails intact. Heat a wok until very hot, then add the oil and swirl to coat the side. Heat over high heat until smoking, then quickly add the ginger, garlic and spring onion and stir-fry for 1 minute. Add the prawns and cook for 2 minutes, or until they are just pink and starting to curl. Remove the prawns from the wok with tongs or a slotted spoon.
2 Put the chilli garlic sauce, tomato sauce, rice wine, vinegar, soy sauce, sugar and cornflour paste in a small jug and whisk together. Pour the sauce into the wok and cook, stirring, for 1–2 minutes, or until it thickens slightly. Return the prawns to the wok for 1–2 minutes, or until heated and cooked through. Garnish with the finely chopped spring onion. Serve immediately with rice or thin egg noodles.

Nutrition per serve: Fat 8.5 g; Protein 40 g; Carbohydrate 12 g; Dietary Fibre 1.5 g; Cholesterol 279.5 mg; 1230 kJ (295 Cal)

Notes: Chinese rice wine has a rich sweetish taste. Use dry sherry if unavailable.

Chinese black vinegar is made from rice and has a sweet, mild taste. It is available in Asian food stores.

Crumbed prawns with ponzu dipping sauce (top), and Sweet chilli prawns

BAKED PRAWNS, TOMATO AND FETA

Prep time: 15 minutes
Cooking time: 45 minutes
Serves 4

2 tablespoons extra virgin olive oil
1 red onion, finely chopped
2 cloves garlic, chopped
1 cup (250 ml) dry white wine
425 g can crushed tomatoes
2 tablespoons chopped fresh oregano
20 raw medium prawns, peeled and deveined, with tails intact
200 g feta, drained and roughly crumbled
3 tablespoons chopped fresh flat-leaf parsley

1 Preheat the oven to moderate 180°C (350°F/Gas 4). Heat the oil in a saucepan over medium–high heat and cook the onion for 1 minute. Add the garlic, wine and tomato and cook for 2 minutes, then reduce the heat and simmer for 15–20 minutes, or until thickened. Cool slightly, then stir in the oregano.
2 Using about half the tomato mixture, divide among four 1 cup (250 ml) gratin dishes. Arrange five prawns in each dish. Spoon in the remaining tomato mixture, then top with feta. Sprinkle with half the parsley.
3 Bake for about 20 minutes, or until browned at the edges and the prawns are cooked through. Sprinkle with the remaining parsley and serve with a Greek salad.

Nutrition per serve: Fat 21 g; Protein 28 g; Carbohydrate 5 g; Dietary Fibre 2 g; Cholesterol 165.5 mg; 1515 kJ (360 Cal)

PRAWN POT PIES

Prep time: 15 minutes
Cooking time: 1 hour
Serves 4

1 kg raw medium prawns
60 g butter
1 leek (white part only), thinly sliced
1 clove garlic, finely chopped
1 tablespoon plain flour
3/4 cup (185 ml) chicken or fish stock
1/2 cup (125 ml) dry white wine
2 cups (500 ml) cream
2 tablespoons lemon juice
1 tablespoon chopped fresh dill
1 tablespoon chopped fresh flat-leaf parsley
1 teaspoon Dijon mustard
1 sheet frozen puff pastry, just thawed
1 egg, lightly beaten

1 Preheat the oven to hot 220°C (425°F/Gas 7). Peel and devein the prawns. Melt the butter in a saucepan over low heat. Cook the leek and garlic for 2 minutes, then add the prawns and cook for 1–2 minutes, or until just pink. Remove the prawns with a slotted spoon and reserve.
2 Stir the flour into the pan and cook for 1 minute. Add the stock and wine, bring to the boil and cook for 10 minutes, or until the liquid has nearly evaporated. Stir in the cream, bring to the boil, then reduce the heat and simmer for 20 minutes, or until the liquid reduces by half. Stir in the lemon juice, herbs and mustard.
3 Using half the sauce, pour an even amount into four 1 cup (250 ml) ramekins. Divide the prawns among the ramekins, then top with the remaining sauce.
4 Cut the pastry into four rounds slightly larger than the rim of the ramekins. Place the pastry rounds over the prawn mixture and press around the edges. Prick the pastry and brush with beaten egg. Bake for 20 minutes, or until the pastry is crisp and golden. Serve with a salad and bread.

Nutrition per serve: Fat 74 g; Protein 33 g; Carbohydrate 16 g; Dietary Fibre 1 g; Cholesterol 446 mg; 3635 kJ (870 Cal)

Baked prawns, tomato and feta (top), and Prawn pot pies

SICHUAN PRAWN AND NOODLE STIR-FRY

Prep time: 20 minutes
Cooking time: 10 minutes
Serves 4

600 g thin fresh rice noodles
1/3 cup (80 ml) peanut oil
20 raw medium prawns, peeled and deveined, with tails intact
1 tablespoon Chinese rice wine
1 cm x 2 cm piece fresh ginger, peeled and thinly shredded
2 cloves garlic, crushed
1–2 small fresh red chillies, seeded and thinly sliced
2 tablespoons chilli bean paste
4 spring onions, thinly sliced on the diagonal
1/2 cup (15 g) fresh coriander leaves

1 Soak the noodles in boiling water for 5 minutes, then drain and refresh under cold running water.
2 Heat a wok over high heat, then add the oil and swirl to coat. Cook the prawns for 1 minute, stirring constantly. Add the wine, ginger, garlic and chilli and cook for a minute. Add the noodles to the wok and stir through gently until mixed together. Add the chilli bean paste and spring onion. Stir over high heat for a further minute. Sprinkle with coriander and serve.

Nutrition per serve: Fat 18.5 g; Protein 22 g; Carbohydrate 35 g; Dietary Fibre 2 g; Cholesterol 127.5 mg; 1675 kJ (400 Cal)

COCONUT SAMBAL PRAWN SKEWERS

Prep time: 25 minutes + 30 minutes soaking + 1 hour refrigeration
Cooking time: 10 minutes
Serves 4

1/3 cup (80 ml) coconut cream
1/4 cup (60 ml) lime juice
2 tablespoons soy sauce
1 tablespoon grated lime rind
2 teaspoons chopped fresh red chilli
1 teaspoon grated palm sugar or soft brown sugar
1/2 teaspoon shrimp paste
4 cloves garlic, crushed
32 raw medium prawns, peeled and deveined, with tails intact
2 teaspoons oil
1 tablespoon chopped fresh coriander
mango chutney, to serve

Coconut sambal
1/4 cup (25 g) desiccated coconut
1/4 cup (40 g) sesame seeds
1/2 teaspoon dried garlic flakes
1/4 teaspoon ground coriander
1/4 teaspoon ground cumin
1/4 cup (40 g) roasted unsalted peanuts, roughly chopped

1 Soak eight bamboo skewers in water for 30 minutes.
2 Combine the coconut cream, lime juice, soy sauce, lime rind, chilli, sugar, shrimp paste and garlic in a bowl and mix until the sugar dissolves.
3 Thread four prawns on each skewer. Place on a non-metallic plate and pour the marinade over them and refrigerate, covered, for 1 hour.
4 To make the sambal, toast the coconut in a dry frying pan for 1–2 minutes, or until golden, then add the sesame seeds, garlic flakes, spices and 1/2 teaspoon salt and cook for about 30 seconds. Remove from the heat and stir in the peanuts. Spoon into a small serving bowl.
5 Heat a chargrill pan or barbecue to high and brush with a little oil. Cook the prawns on both sides for 2–3 minutes, or until pink and cooked. Place on a platter and sprinkle with coriander. Serve with the sambal and chutney.

Nutrition per serve: Fat 20 g; Protein 32 g; Carbohydrate 4.5 g; Dietary Fibre 3.5 g; Cholesterol 184.5 mg; 1370 kJ (330 Cal)

Sichuan prawn and noodle stir-fry (top), and Coconut sambal prawn skewers

PRAWN LAKSA

Prep time: 30 minutes
Cooking time: 35 minutes
Serves 4–6

11/2 tablespoons coriander
    seeds
1 tablespoon cumin seeds
1 teaspoon ground turmeric
1 onion, roughly chopped
1 cm x 3 cm piece fresh
    ginger, peeled and roughly
    chopped
3 cloves garlic
3 stems lemon grass (white
    part only), sliced
6 candlenuts or macadamias
    (see Notes)
4–6 small fresh red chillies
2–3 teaspoons shrimp paste
    (see Notes)
1 litre chicken stock
1/4 cup (60 ml) oil
3 cups (750 ml) coconut milk
4 fresh kaffir lime leaves
21/2 tablespoons lime juice
2 tablespoons fish sauce
2 tablespoons grated palm
    sugar or soft brown sugar
750 g raw medium prawns,
    peeled and deveined, with
    tails intact
250 g dried rice vermicelli
    noodles (see Notes)
1 cup (90 g) bean sprouts
4 fried tofu puffs, cut into
    julienne strips (see Notes)
3 tablespoons roughly
    chopped fresh Vietnamese
    mint (see Notes)
2/3 cup (20 g) fresh
    coriander leaves
lime wedges, to serve

1 Roast the coriander
seeds in a dry saucepan
or small frying pan
over medium heat for
1–2 minutes, or until
fragrant, tossing the pan
constantly to prevent
them burning. Grind
finely in a mortar and
pestle or a spice grinder.
Repeat the process with
the cumin seeds.

2 Place all the spices,
onion, ginger, garlic,
lemon grass, candlenuts,
chillies and shrimp paste
in a food processor or
blender. Add about
1/2 cup (125 ml) of
the stock and blend to
a fine paste.

3 Heat the oil in a large
saucepan over low heat
and gently cook the
paste for 3–5 minutes,
stirring constantly to
prevent the paste
burning or sticking to
the bottom of the pan.
Pour in the remaining
stock and bring to the
boil, then reduce the
heat and simmer for
15 minutes, or until
reduced slightly.

4 Add the coconut
milk, lime leaves, lime
juice, fish sauce and
palm sugar and simmer
for 5 minutes. Add the
prawns and simmer for
2 minutes, or until the
prawns are pink and
cooked through. Do
not bring to the boil or
cover with a lid or the
coconut milk will split.

5 Meanwhile, soak the
rice vermicelli in a bowl
of boiling water for

5 minutes, or until
softened. Drain and
divide among large
serving bowls along with
most of the bean sprouts.
Ladle hot soup over the
noodles and garnish each
bowl with some tofu,
mint, coriander leaves
and the remaining bean
sprouts. Serve with some
lime wedges for your
guests to squeeze over
the laksa.

Nutrition per serve (6): Fat 39 g;
Protein 20 g; Carbohydrate 50 g;
Dietary Fibre 4.5 g; Cholesterol
94.5 mg; 2615 kJ (625 Cal)

Notes: Candlenuts are large
cream-coloured nuts, similar
to macadamias in shape. They
cannot be eaten raw as the oil
is toxic unless cooked.

Shrimp paste is a pungent paste
made from fermented prawns.
To reduce the smell, it should be
wrapped in plastic and stored
in the refrigerator in an airtight
container. It is available from
Asian food stores.

Dried rice vermicelli noodles are
packaged in blocks and are very
thin translucent noodles.

Fried tofu puffs are cubes of tofu
that have been deep-fried to
become golden and puffed.

Vietnamese mint has a flavour
that resembles coriander but
is slightly sharper. Despite the
name, it does not belong to the
mint family. Vietnamese mint is
available from Asian food stores,
but if you can't find it, use fresh
coriander instead.

Prawn laksa

CREAMY TOMATO AND PRAWN PASTA

Prep time: 25 minutes
Cooking time: 15 minutes
Serves 4

400 g dried egg tagliatelle
1 tablespoon olive oil
3 cloves garlic, finely chopped
20 raw medium prawns, peeled and deveined, with tails intact
550 g Roma tomatoes, diced
2 tablespoons thinly sliced fresh basil
150 ml white wine
1/3 cup (80 ml) cream
baby basil leaves, to garnish

1 Cook the pasta in a large saucepan of boiling water until *al dente*. Drain and keep warm, reserving 2 tablespoons of the cooking water.
2 Meanwhile, heat the oil and garlic in a large frying pan over low heat for 1–2 minutes. Increase the heat to medium, add the prawns and cook for 3–5 minutes, stirring frequently until cooked. Remove the prawns and keep warm.
3 Add the tomato and sliced basil and stir for 3 minutes, or until the tomato is soft. Pour in the wine and cream, bring to the boil and simmer for 2 minutes.

4 Purée the sauce in a blender, return to the pan, then add the reserved pasta water and bring to a simmer. Stir in the prawns until heated through. Toss through the pasta and serve garnished with basil.

Nutrition per serve: Fat 14.5 g; Protein 32 g; Carbohydrate 74 g; Dietary Fibre 4.5 g; Cholesterol 169.5 mg; 2435 kJ (580 Cal)

PRAWN AND BEAN SALAD

Prep time: 30 minutes +
  8 hours soaking
Cooking time: 50 minutes
Serves 4

1 cup (200 g) dried cannellini beans
2 red capsicums, cut into large flattish pieces
300 g green beans, trimmed
1/2 loaf (150 g) day-old ciabatta bread or other crusty loaf
1/3 cup (80 ml) olive oil
1 large clove garlic, finely chopped
1 kg raw medium prawns, peeled and deveined, with tails intact
11/2 cups (30 g) fresh flat-leaf parsley

Dressing
1/4 cup (60 ml) lemon juice
1/4 cup (60 ml) olive oil
2 tablespoons capers, chopped
1 teaspoon sugar (optional)

1 Soak the cannellini beans in a large bowl of cold water for 8 hours.
2 Drain then rinse the beans well, transfer to a saucepan, cover with cold water and cook for 20–30 minutes, or until tender. Drain, rinse under cold water, drain again and put in a large serving bowl.
3 Cook the capsicum, skin-side-up, under a hot grill until the skin blackens and blisters. Cool in a plastic bag, then peel. Cut into strips, and add to the bowl.
4 Cook the green beans in a saucepan of boiling water for 3–4 minutes, or until tender. Drain and add to the serving bowl. Cut the bread into six slices, then cut each slice in four. Heat 1/4 cup (60 ml) of the oil in a frying pan and cook the bread over medium heat on each side until golden. Remove from the pan.
5 Heat the remaining oil in the frying pan, add the garlic and prawns and cook for 1–2 minutes, or until the prawns are pink and cooked. Add to the salad with the parsley.
6 Combine the dressing ingredients, then season. Toss the dressing and bread through the salad.

Nutrition per serve: Fat 29 g; Protein 43 g; Carbohydrate 42 g; Dietary Fibre 13.5 g; Cholesterol 186 mg; 2495 kJ (595 Cal)

Creamy tomato and prawn pasta (top), and Prawn and bean salad

PRAWN AND RICE NOODLE SALAD

Prep time: 25 minutes +
10 minutes soaking
Cooking time: 5 minutes
Serves 4

250 g rice stick noodles
700 g medium cooked
prawns, peeled and
deveined, with tails intact
1 carrot, coarsely grated
1 small Lebanese cucumber,
thinly sliced
1 cup (30 g) fresh coriander
leaves
1/2 cup (80 g) roasted
unsalted peanuts, chopped
1/4 cup (50 g) crisp fried
shallots (see Note)

Dressing
1/2 cup (125 ml) rice vinegar
1 tablespoon grated palm
sugar or soft brown sugar
1 clove garlic, finely chopped
2 fresh red chillies, finely
chopped
1/4 cup (60 ml) fish sauce
1/4 cup (60 ml) lime juice
2 tablespoons peanut oil

1 Soak the noodles
in boiling water in a
large heatproof bowl for
10 minutes. Drain, rinse
under cold water to
cool, and drain again.
Place in a serving bowl.
2 Add the prawns,
carrot, cucumber and
coriander to the bowl
and toss well.
3 To make the dressing,
combine the vinegar,
sugar and garlic in a

small saucepan and
bring to the boil, then
reduce the heat and
simmer for 3 minutes
to slightly reduce the
liquid. Transfer to a
bowl and add the chilli,
fish sauce and lime juice.
Slowly whisk in the oil,
and season to taste.
4 Toss the dressing
through the salad, then
scatter with the peanuts
and crisp fried shallots
and serve.

Nutrition per serve: Fat 20 g;
Protein 25 g; Carbohydrate 63 g;
Dietary Fibre 3 g; Cholesterol
130.5 mg; 2240 kJ (535 Cal)

Note: Crisp fried shallots are red
Asian shallot flakes used as a
garnish in Southeast Asia. They
are available from Asian food
stores in packets or tubs.

SALT AND PEPPER PRAWNS

Prep time: 20 minutes +
30 minutes refrigeration
Cooking time: 5 minutes
Serves 4–6

1 egg white
2 cloves garlic, crushed
1 kg raw medium prawns,
peeled and deveined, with
tails intact
1 tablespoon vegetable oil
1 long red chilli, sliced on the
diagonal
1/2 cup (90 g) rice flour
1 tablespoon ground
Sichuan peppercorns
2 teaspoons ground sea salt

1 teaspoon ground white
pepper
1 teaspoon caster sugar
peanut oil, for deep-frying

1 Combine the egg
white with the garlic in a
bowl and add the prawns.
Stir to coat, cover and
refrigerate for 30 minutes.
2 Meanwhile, heat the
vegetable oil in a small
frying pan until hot,
add the chilli and cook,
stirring, for 1 minute.
Remove from the pan
and drain on paper
towels.
3 Place the rice flour,
ground peppercorns, salt,
white pepper and sugar
in a bowl and combine.
4 Fill a deep heavy-
based saucepan or deep-
fryer one third full of oil
and heat to 180°C
(350°F), or until a cube
of bread browns in
15 seconds. Coat each
prawn in the flour,
shaking off any excess,
and deep-fry in batches
for about 1 minute or
until lightly golden and
cooked through. Drain
on paper towels and
season. Top with chilli
and serve with steamed
rice and green vegetables.
Serve immediately.

Nutrition per serve (6): Fat 15 g;
Protein 19 g; Carbohydrate 14 g;
Dietary Fibre 1 g; Cholesterol
124 mg; 1110 kJ (265 Cal)

Prawn and rice noodle
salad (top), and Salt and
pepper prawns

PRAWNS WITH ALMONDS AND BROWN BUTTER

Prep time: 10 minutes
Cooking time: 15 minutes
Serves 4

100 g butter
1 large leek (white part only), thinly sliced
2 cloves garlic, crushed
1 kg raw large prawns, peeled and deveined, with tails intact
30 g flaked almonds
2 tablespoons chopped fresh flat-leaf parsley
500 g English spinach, washed

1 Melt 25 g of the butter in a frying pan. Add the leek and cook over low heat for 3–4 minutes, or until soft. Add the garlic and prawns and sauté for 2–3 minutes, or until pink. Remove from the pan.

2 Heat the remaining butter in the same frying pan and when it turns nutty brown (about 1 1/2–2 minutes), add the almonds. Cook, stirring, until golden. Return the prawns and leek to the pan, then add the parsley and stir until the prawns are cooked through.

Prawns with almonds and brown butter (top), and Prawn, prosciutto and rocket salad

3 Place the spinach in a large saucepan and heat to medium. As the spinach on the bottom starts to wilt, lift it to the top, sprinkling with water if the spinach is sticking. Continue tossing until all the spinach has wilted. Divide the spinach among four serving plates and arrange the prawns on top. Serve with steamed rice.

Nutrition per serve: Fat 24 g; Protein 30.5 g; Carbohydrate 2 g; Dietary Fibre 5 g; Cholesterol 244 mg; 1435 kJ (345 Cal)

PRAWN, PROSCIUTTO AND ROCKET SALAD

Prep time: 15 minutes
Cooking time:
    1 hour 30 minutes
Serves 4

4 Roma tomatoes, quartered lengthways
1 clove garlic, chopped
1/3 cup (80 ml) olive oil
8 slices prosciutto
20 raw medium prawns, peeled, deveined and cut in half lengthways
2 teaspoons balsamic vinegar
2 avocados, stone removed and thinly sliced
60 g baby rocket leaves

1 Preheat the oven to very slow 140°C

(275°F/Gas 1). Place the tomato quarters in a bowl and toss with the garlic, 1 tablespoon of the oil and some salt and pepper. Place the tomato quarters on a baking tray and roast for 1 1/2 hours. Remove from the oven.

2 Lightly brush the prosciutto with a little of the remaining olive oil. Heat a non-stick frying pan over medium–high heat. When hot, add the prosciutto in two batches, cooking for 3–4 minutes each side until it starts to become crisp. Drain on paper towels to remove any excess oil, then break into shards.

3 Heat a chargrill pan until it is hot, lightly oil the pan, then cook the prawns in two batches for 2 minutes each side. Season well and transfer to a large serving bowl.

4 Combine the rest of the olive oil with the balsamic vinegar. To assemble the salad, place the tomato, prosciutto, avocado and rocket in the bowl with the prawns. Drizzle with 1 tablespoon of the dressing, then gently toss together. Drizzle with the remaining dressing and serve.

Nutrition per serve: Fat 39.5 g; Protein 28 g; Carbohydrate 2 g; Dietary Fibre 2.5 g; Cholesterol 149 mg; 1980 kJ (475 Cal)

USING COOKED PRAWNS

Pre-cooked prawns are a convenient way to buy prawns. Serve them with a simple squeeze of lemon or, as shown below, add a few well-chosen ingredients for something more special.

PRAWN NICOISE SALAD

Peel and devein 750 g cooked large prawns, leaving the tails intact. Chill until needed. Boil 300 g unpeeled small Pontiac potatoes for 20–25 minutes, or until just tender. Drain, cool, then cut into 1 cm slices. Blanch 150 g baby green beans, then plunge into iced water. Cut four Roma tomatoes into quarters or eighths, depending on their size. Hard-boil 12 quail eggs (2–3 minutes) or four hen eggs, drain, shell and cut in half (quarters for hen eggs). Separate the leaves of a butter lettuce and arrange on a platter. Top with the potato, beans, prawns, tomato, eggs, 2 tablespoons capers and 10 baby olives. Mix 1/3 cup (80 ml) olive oil with 2 tablespoons balsamic vinegar, 1 clove crushed garlic and 4 chopped anchovies in a screw-top jar, shake, then pour over the salad. Sprinkle 2 tablespoons chopped fresh chervil or flat-leaf parsley over the top, season, then serve. Serves 4.

BRUSCHETTA

Peel and devein 24 cooked medium prawns. Slice a crusty Italian loaf into eight 1.5 cm slices. Toast the slices under a hot grill, then spread each slice with some good-quality ready-made pesto. Divide 100 g baby rocket leaves over the pesto, top each piece with 3 prawns and scatter each with 2 teaspoons crumbled feta. Drizzle with extra virgin olive oil and season to taste. Makes 8.

CONTEMPORARY PRAWN COCKTAIL

Preheat the oven to moderately hot 200°C (400°F/Gas 6). Peel and devein 20 cooked medium prawns and divide among four plates, along with 80 g frisée and one sliced mango. Chill. To make the dressing, cut two Roma tomatoes into quarters, place on a baking tray with 3 unpeeled garlic cloves and sprinkle with 1 1/2 teaspoons sugar. Roast for 25 minutes, then cool slightly and peel the garlic. Transfer the tomato and garlic to a food processor and blend until smooth. Mix with 1/2 cup (125 g) whole-egg mayonnaise, 2 tablespoons lime juice and 1 1/2 tablespoons chopped fresh basil. Drizzle over the salad, then season. Serve with lime wedges. Serves 4.

PRAWN CAESAR SALAD

Preheat the oven to moderately hot 190°C (375°F/Gas 5). Peel and devein 500 g cooked medium prawns. To make the dressing, put 2 tablespoons grated Parmesan, 1 tablespoon lemon juice, 1 teaspoon Worcestershire sauce, 2 egg yolks, 1/2 teaspoon Dijon mustard, 1 small clove garlic and 6 anchovy fillets in a food processor. Process until smooth, then, with the motor running, add 1/2 cup (125 ml) olive oil in a slow, thin stream until thick and creamy. Tear the leaves of two baby cos lettuces into bite-sized pieces and put in a large bowl with the prawns. Cut a small baguette into 1 cm slices. Brush both sides with oil, then bake for 5–10 minutes, or until golden. Rub each slice with a cut clove of garlic and keep warm. Grill 3 rashers of bacon until crisp. Break into shards. Mix half the dressing with the prawns and lettuce, and toss well. Arrange the salad in four bowls, then divide two finely grated hard-boiled eggs, bacon and shaved Parmesan among them. Serve with garlic toast and dressing. Serves 4.

From left: Prawn niçoise salad, Bruschetta, Contemporary prawn cocktail, and Prawn Caesar salad.

PRAWN TOASTS

Prep time: 25 minutes +
  1 hour refrigeration
Cooking time: 10 minutes
Makes 16

16 raw large prawns
1 egg white
2 tablespoons cornflour
1 tablespoon Chinese rice
  wine
1 small fresh red chilli,
  seeded and finely chopped
1 small clove garlic, crushed
1/4 cup (60 ml) tomato sauce
1 tablespoon hoisin sauce
1 teaspoon Worcestershire
  sauce
8 slices of white bread
oil, for shallow-frying
sliced spring onion, to garnish

1 Peel and devein the prawns, leaving the tails intact. Cut down the back of each prawn to form a butterfly. Place each prawn between two sheets of plastic wrap and beat to form a cutlet.
2 Place the egg white, cornflour, rice wine and 1/2 teaspoon salt in a bowl and whisk until the batter thickens a little. Evenly coat the prawns in the batter. Cover and refrigerate for 1 hour.
3 To make the barbecue sauce, combine the chilli, garlic, and tomato, hoisin and Worcestershire sauces in a small bowl.

Prawn toasts (top), and
Prawn pilau

4 Remove the crusts from the bread and cut each slice of bread in half lengthways. Press each prawn into a piece of bread and hold down firmly for 5 seconds.
5 Fill a frying pan or wok one third full of oil. Cook the toasts in batches for 2 minutes, or until golden brown. Garnish with the spring onion slices and serve with the barbecue sauce.

Nutrition per toast: Fat 4 g;
Protein 5 g; Carbohydrate 8.5 g;
Dietary Fibre 0.5 g; Cholesterol
28.5 mg; 380 kJ (90 Cal)

PRAWN PILAU

Prep time: 20 minutes
Cooking time: 25 minutes
Serves 4–6

2 cups (400 g) basmati rice
60 g butter
1 onion, finely chopped
2 cloves garlic, finely chopped
1 cm x 4 cm piece fresh
  ginger, peeled and grated
1 fresh green chilli, finely
  chopped
3 teaspoons coriander seeds
1 teaspoon ground turmeric
2 cardamom pods, cracked
1 kg raw medium prawns,
  peeled and deveined, with
  tails intact
1/2 cup (80 g) raw cashew
  nuts
1/3 cup (80 ml) lemon juice
1/2 cup (25 g) chopped fresh
  coriander leaves

1 Rinse the rice under cold water until the water runs clear. Drain well. Melt 30 g of the butter over low heat in a large saucepan; add the onion and cook for 3 minutes, or until soft. Add the garlic, ginger, chilli, coriander seeds and turmeric and cook for 2 minutes.
2 Add the rice to the saucepan and cook for 1 minute, then add the cardamom pods and 1 litre water. Bring to the boil, then reduce the heat and simmer, covered, for 10 minutes, or until the rice is tender. Remove from the heat and leave, covered, for 5 minutes to steam.
3 Melt the remaining butter in a frying pan and cook the prawns and cashews over high heat for 3–4 minutes, or until the prawns are pink and cooked through. Add both to the pan with the rice, then add the lemon juice and coriander and stir everything together. Season to taste with salt and pepper, then serve.

Nutrition per serve (6): Fat 15.5 g;
Protein 25 g; Carbohydrate 57 g;
Dietary Fibre 2 g; Cholesterol
147.5 mg; 1950 kJ (465 Cal)

GARLIC PRAWNS

Prep time: 15 minutes
Cooking time: 20 minutes
Serves 4

20 raw medium prawns
350 ml olive oil
10 cloves garlic, crushed
2 fresh large green chillies,
    seeded and thinly sliced
    on the diagonal
2 tablespoons chopped
    fresh flat-leaf parsley
2 spring onions, thinly sliced

1 Peel and devein the prawns, keeping the tails intact. Preheat the oven to moderately hot 200°C (400°F/Gas 6). Place four cast iron pots or deep ovenproof dishes, 10–12 cm in diameter, on a flat baking tray.
2 Pour one quarter of the oil into each dish, then divide half the garlic among the pots, reserving the other half. Put the tray into the oven and heat the oil for 10–12 minutes, or until the oil bubbles and is very hot.
3 Carefully remove the tray from the oven and place 5 prawns in each dish with some chilli and the remaining garlic. Season with salt and pepper; then gently toss the ingredients together. Return to the oven for a further 5 minutes, or until the prawns are pink and cooked through.

Carefully remove the pots from the oven and sprinkle each pot with parsley and spring onion. Season to taste and serve with crusty bread.

Nutrition per serve: Fat 35 g; Protein 19 g; Carbohydrate 1.5 g; Dietary Fibre 2 g; Cholesterol 127.5 mg; 1630 kJ (390 Cal)

Note: This is the traditional way to make garlic prawns, but they can be made successfully in a cast iron frying pan (with a flameproof handle) in the oven or on the stove top.

PRAWN, POTATO AND CORN CHOWDER

Prep time: 25 minutes
Cooking time: 40 minutes
Serves 4–6

600 g raw medium prawns
3 corn cobs, husks removed
1 tablespoon olive oil
2 leeks (white part only),
    finely chopped
2 cloves garlic, crushed
650 g potatoes, cut into
    1.5 cm cubes
3 cups (750 ml) fish or
    chicken stock
1 1/2 cups (375 ml) milk
1 cup (250 ml) cream
pinch of cayenne pepper
3 tablespoons finely
    chopped fresh flat-leaf
    parsley

1 Peel and devein the prawns, then chop them into 1.5 cm pieces.

2 Cut the kernels from the corn cobs. Heat the oil in a large saucepan and add the leek. Cook over medium–low heat for about 5 minutes, or until soft and lightly golden. Add the garlic and cook for 30 seconds, then add the corn, potato, stock and milk.
3 Bring to the boil, then reduce the heat and simmer, partially covered, for about 20 minutes, or until the potato is soft but still holds its shape (it will break down slightly). Remove the lid and simmer for a further 10 minutes to allow the soup to thicken. Reduce the heat to low. Put 2 cups (500 ml) of the soup in a blender and blend until very smooth.
4 Return the blended soup to the saucepan and add the prawns. Increase the heat to medium and simmer for 2 minutes, or until the prawns are pink and cooked through. Stir in the cream, cayenne and 2 tablespoons of the parsley. Season with salt, then serve garnished with the remaining parsley.

Nutrition per serve (6): Fat 24.5 g; Protein 19 g; Carbohydrate 27 g; Dietary Fibre 4 g; Cholesterol 139.5 mg; 1690 kJ (405 Cal)

Garlic prawns (top), and Prawn, potato and corn chowder

PRAWN SAN CHOY BAU

Prep time: 20 minutes
Cooking time: 5 minutes
Serves 4–6

1 iceberg lettuce
1 kg raw medium prawns, peeled and deveined, or 500 g raw prawn meat
1 tablespoon oil
1 teaspoon sesame oil
2 spring onions, finely chopped
2 cloves garlic, crushed
1 cm x 2 cm piece fresh ginger, peeled and grated
120 g drained water chestnuts, chopped
1 tablespoon chopped fresh red chilli
1 cup (185 g) cooked white rice
1 cup (90 g) bean sprouts, trimmed
1/2 cup (25 g) chopped fresh coriander leaves
2 tablespoons soy sauce
2 tablespoons oyster sauce
2 tablespoons lime juice
1/4 cup (60 ml) hoisin sauce

1 Wash the lettuce and separate the leaves. Shake off any excess water and drain on paper towels.
2 If the prawns are large, cut them into smaller pieces. Heat a wok over high heat, add the oils, swirl to coat, then add the spring onion, garlic and ginger.

Prawn san choy bau (top), and Spiced prawn pakoras

Cook for 30 seconds then add the prawn meat, water chestnuts and chilli, season with salt and cracked black pepper and continue stir-frying for 2 minutes. Add the rice, sprouts and coriander and stir until combined.
3 Add the soy sauce, oyster sauce and lime juice, then remove from the heat. Transfer the mixture to a serving bowl. Place the dry lettuce cups on a plate and spoon the prawn mixture into each one. Serve with hoisin sauce.

Nutrition per serve (6): Fat 5 g; Protein 20 g; Carbohydrate 19 g; Dietary Fibre 2.5 g; Cholesterol 124 mg; 845 kJ (200 Cal)

SPICED PRAWN PAKORAS

Prep time: 20 minutes
Cooking time: 10 minutes
Makes 16

3/4 cup (85 g) besan (chickpea flour)
1/2 teaspoon baking powder
1/4 teaspoon ground turmeric
1 teaspoon ground coriander
1/2 teaspoon ground cumin
1/2 teaspoon chilli powder
oil, for deep-frying
1 tablespoon egg white
16 raw medium prawns, peeled and deveined, with tails intact

Dipping sauce
1 cup (250 g) plain yoghurt
3 tablespoons chopped fresh coriander leaves
1 teaspoon ground cumin
garam masala, to sprinkle

1 Sift the besan, baking powder and spices into a large bowl and season with a little salt. Make a well in the centre, gradually add 1 cup (250 ml) water and stir gently until mixed.
2 Fill a large heavy-based saucepan one third full of oil and heat to 160°C (315°F), or until a cube of bread browns in 30–35 seconds. Beat the egg white until firm peaks form, and fold into the batter. Using the tail as a handle, dip the prawns into the batter, then lower gently into the oil.
3 Cook about four prawns at a time, without overcrowding the pan. Cook for 2 minutes, until the batter is lightly golden; it won't become really crisp. Drain on crumpled paper towels.
4 To make the dipping sauce, combine the yoghurt, coriander and cumin. Sprinkle with the garam masala. Serve with the prawns.

Nutrition per pakora: Fat 8 g; Protein 6 g; Carbohydrate 4 g; Dietary Fibre 0.5 g; Cholesterol 28.5 mg; 460 kJ (110 Cal)

PRAWN TARTLETS WITH SALSA VERDE

Prep time: 30 minutes +
50 minutes refrigeration
Cooking time: 30 minutes
Serves 4

Pastry
11/2 cups (185 g) plain flour
90 g butter, chopped
2 tablespoons drained semi-
dried tomatoes, finely
chopped
11/2–2 tablespoons cold
water

Salsa verde
1 cup (20 g) tightly packed
fresh flat-leaf parsley
4 tablespoons chopped
fresh mint
3 tablespoons fresh basil
2 tablespoons chopped
fresh chives
1 clove garlic
1/3 cup (80 ml) lemon juice
1/4 cup (30 g) capers, rinsed
5 anchovy fillets
1/2 cup (125 ml) olive oil

Filling
2 Roma tomatoes, seeded
and diced
2 tablespoons lemon juice
1 tablespoon finely chopped
fresh basil
2 tablespoons olive oil
3 spring onions, finely
chopped
2 teaspoons grated lemon
rind
720 g raw medium prawns,
peeled and deveined

1 To make the pastry,
sift the flour into a large
bowl and add the butter.
Rub the butter into the
flour with your fingertips
until it resembles fine
breadcrumbs. Stir in the
semi-dried tomatoes.
Make a well in the
centre, add the water
and mix with a flat-
bladed knife, using a
cutting action until the
mixture comes together
in beads—you might need
to add a little more water
if the dough is too dry.
Gently gather the dough
together and lift out
onto a lightly floured
work surface. Shape the
dough into four rounds,
cover in plastic wrap and
refrigerate for 20 minutes.
2 Roll each round into
a circle large enough
to line a 12 cm loose-
bottomed tart tin. Line
the tins with pastry,
cover with plastic wrap
and refrigerate for a
further 30 minutes.
3 Preheat the oven to
moderately hot 200°C
(400°F/Gas 6). Prick the
base of the pastry cases
with a fork, line with a
small piece of crumpled
baking paper and fill
with baking beads or
dried beans. Blind bake
the pastry cases for
10 minutes, remove
the baking beads and
paper, and cook for a
further 5–10 minutes,
or until the base is dry.
Cool for 5 minutes, then
remove the pastry cases
and place them on a
wire rack.
4 To make the salsa
verde, place the herbs
and garlic in a food
processor and process
for 30 seconds, or until
combined. Add the
lemon juice, capers and
anchovies and process
until mixed. With the
motor running, slowly
add the oil in a thin
stream and process until
the mixture is smooth.
5 To make the filling,
combine the diced
tomato with the lemon
juice, basil and
1 tablespoon of the oil.
6 In a separate bowl,
combine the remaining
oil with the spring onion
and lemon rind. Add the
prawns and stir to coat.
Heat a lightly oiled
chargrill or barbecue
to very hot. Add the
drained prawns and cook
in batches over high heat
for 4 minutes, turning
frequently until pink and
cooked through. Season.
7 To serve, place the
pastry cases on serving
plates, fill with the
tomato mixture, top
with the prawns and
drizzle with the salsa
verde. Serve warm or at
room temperature with a
rocket salad.

Nutrition per serve: Fat 56 g;
Protein 27 g; Carbohydrate 39 g;
Dietary Fibre 4 g; Cholesterol
195.5 mg; 3180 kJ (760 Cal)

Prawn tartlets with
salsa verde

HONEY PRAWNS

Prep time: 20 minutes
Cooking time: 15 minutes
Serves 4

16 raw large prawns
cornflour, for dusting
oil, for deep-frying
3 egg whites, lightly beaten
2 tablespoons cornflour, extra
2 tablespoons oil, extra
1/4 cup (90 g) honey
2 tablespoons sesame
   seeds, toasted

1 Peel and devein the prawns, leaving the tails intact. Pat them dry and lightly dust with the cornflour, shaking off any excess. Fill a large heavy-based saucepan or wok one third full of oil and heat to 180°C (350°F), or until a cube of bread dropped in the oil browns in 15 seconds.
2 Beat the egg whites in a clean dry bowl until soft peaks form. Add the extra cornflour and some salt and gently whisk until combined and smooth. Using the tail as a handle, dip the prawns in the batter, then slowly lower them into the oil. Cook in batches for 3–4 minutes, or until crisp and golden and the prawns are cooked. Remove with a slotted spoon, then drain on

Honey prawns (top), and
Piri piri prawns

crumpled paper towels and keep warm.
3 Heat the extra oil and honey in a saucepan over medium heat for 2–3 minutes, or until bubbling. Place the prawns on a serving plate and pour on the honey sauce. Sprinkle with the sesame seeds and serve immediately with steamed rice.

Nutrition per serve: Fat 25.5 g; Protein 20 g; Carbohydrate 25 g; Dietary Fibre 0.5 g; Cholesterol 113 mg; 1695 kJ (405 Cal)

PIRI PIRI PRAWNS

Prep time: 25 minutes +
   30 minutes marinating
Cooking time: 15 minutes
Serves 4

1 kg raw large prawns
4 long fresh red chillies,
   deseeded
3/4 cup (185 ml) white wine
   vinegar
2 large cloves garlic, chopped
6–8 small fresh red chillies,
   chopped
1/2 cup (125 ml) olive oil
150 g mixed lettuce leaves

1 Remove the heads from the prawns. Slice the prawns down the back without cutting right through, leaving the tail intact. Open the prawn out and remove the vein. Place the prawns in a non-metallic

bowl, cover and refrigerate until needed.
2 Place the long chillies in a saucepan with the vinegar and simmer over medium–high heat for 5 minutes, or until the chillies are soft. Cool slightly. Transfer the chillies and 1/4 cup (60 ml) of the vinegar to a food processor (reserve the rest of the vinegar), then add the garlic and chopped chilli and blend until smooth.
3 With the motor running, gradually add the oil and remaining vinegar and process until well combined. Coat the prawns in the sauce, then cover and keep in the fridge for 30 minutes.
4 Heat a chargrill pan or barbecue to high. Lightly oil the pan, then cook the prawns, basting with the marinade, for 2–3 minutes each side, or until cooked. Boil the remaining marinade in a small saucepan, then reduce the heat to low and simmer for 3–4 minutes, or until slightly thickened and reduced. Divide the lettuce among four plates and arrange the prawns on top. Serve immediately with the remaining sauce.

Nutrition per serve: Fat 27 g; Protein 26.5 g; Carbohydrate 1 g; Dietary Fibre 1.5 g; Cholesterol 186 mg; 1505 kJ (360 Cal)

VIETNAMESE PRAWN ROLLS

Prep time: 25 minutes
Cooking time: Nil
Makes 12

2/3 cup (170 ml) lime juice
2 teaspoons grated lime rind
1/3 cup (80 ml) sweet chilli
   sauce
2 teaspoons fish sauce
2 teaspoons grated palm
   sugar or soft brown sugar
12 x 15 cm rice paper
   wrappers
12 cooked medium prawns,
   peeled and halved
   lengthways
1 small carrot, cut into 5 cm
   long julienne strips
1 small Lebanese cucumber,
   cut into 5 cm batons
1/2 avocado, sliced
3 tablespoons fresh
   coriander leaves
2 tablespoons torn fresh
   Vietnamese mint
5 spring onions, thinly sliced
   on the diagonal

1 Combine the lime juice and rind, sweet chilli sauce, fish sauce and sugar in a small bowl.
2 Working with one rice paper wrapper at a time, dip a wrapper in a bowl of warm water for 10 seconds to soften, then lay out on a flat surface. Place 2 prawn halves and a little of each remaining ingredient at one end of the wrapper, then drizzle with 1 teaspoon of the sauce.

Fold in the sides and roll up tightly. Serve with the remaining sauce for dipping.

Nutrition per roll: Fat 2.5 g; Protein 2 g; Carbohydrate 5 g; Dietary Fibre 1 g; Cholesterol 11.5 mg; 225 kJ (55 Cal)

PRAWNS IN CHINESE PANCAKES

Prep time: 20 minutes
   + 10 minutes marinating
Cooking time: 15 minutes
Makes 24

24 raw medium prawns,
   peeled and deveined
1/3 cup (80 ml) Chinese rice
   wine or dry sherry
2 tablespoons soy sauce
2 teaspoons sesame oil
2 tablespoons vegetable oil
4 cloves garlic, finely chopped
1 cm x 4 cm piece fresh
   ginger, peeled and finely
   shredded
120–160 ml Chinese plum
   sauce
2 teaspoons chilli sauce
2 spring onions, finely
   chopped
24 Chinese pancakes (see
   Note)
1 small Lebanese cucumber,
   peeled, seeded and cut
   into thin 5 cm long strips
12 garlic chives, cut into
   5 cm lengths

1 Place the prawns in a non-metallic bowl with the rice wine, soy sauce and sesame oil and

marinate for at least 10 minutes.
2 Heat a wok over high heat, add the vegetable oil and swirl to coat. Add the garlic and ginger and sauté for 1–2 minutes. Use a slotted spoon or tongs to remove the prawns from the marinade and add them to the wok. Reserve the marinade. Stir the prawns for 2 minutes, or until they start to turn pink, then add the plum sauce, chilli sauce and the reserved marinade. Stir-fry for 2–3 minutes, or until the prawns are cooked, curled and slightly glazed. Remove from the heat and stir in the spring onion.
3 Place the pancakes in a non-stick frying pan over medium heat for 1 minute, or until warm.
4 To assemble, put a prawn, a few slices of cucumber and a few chive pieces on each pancake, spoon on some sauce, then fold over. Serve immediately.

Nutrition per pancake: Fat 2 g; Protein 4 g; Carbohydrate 7 g; Dietary Fibre 0.5 g; Cholesterol 23.5 mg; 283 kJ (67.5 Cal)

Note: Buy the pancakes, traditionally used for Peking duck, in the freezer of Asian food stores.

Vietnamese prawn rolls (top), and Prawns in Chinese pancakes

PRAWN, RICOTTA AND SPINACH PASTA

Prep time: 15 minutes
Cooking time: 10 minutes
Serves 4

3 firm ripe tomatoes, peeled, seeded and finely chopped
1/2 cup (125 ml) extra virgin olive oil
1/2 cup (125 ml) balsamic vinegar
3 cloves garlic, finely chopped
3 tablespoons finely chopped fresh basil
500 g penne rigate
1 tablespoon olive oil
800 g raw medium prawns, peeled and deveined, with tails intact
100 g baby English spinach leaves
200 g firm ricotta, crumbled
2 tablespoons shaved Parmesan

1 Combine the tomato, extra virgin olive oil, 2 tablespoons of the vinegar, 1 clove of the garlic and 2 tablespoons of the basil.

2 Cook the pasta in a large saucepan of boiling water until *al dente*. Drain and keep warm.

3 Meanwhile, heat the olive oil in a frying pan over high heat, stir in the remaining garlic, then add the prawns and cook over high heat for 1–2 minutes, or until the prawns turn pink. Add the remaining vinegar and basil and cook for 1–2 minutes, or until the liquid has reduced and the prawns are cooked and slightly glazed. Stir in the spinach until just wilted. Season.

4 Toss together everything except the cheeses. Divide among bowls and top with the ricotta and Parmesan.

Nutrition per serve: Fat 41 g; Protein 43 g; Carbohydrate 92 g; Dietary Fibre 8.5 g; Cholesterol 176 mg; 3830 kJ (915 Cal)

PRAWN AND SWEET POTATO FRITTERS

Prep time: 20 minutes
Cooking time: 15 minutes
Makes 24

1 kg raw medium prawns, peeled, deveined and chopped
400 g orange sweet potato, peeled and coarsely grated
4 spring onions, chopped
1 clove garlic, crushed
2 teaspoons finely chopped fresh ginger
3 tablespoons chopped fresh coriander leaves
1/2 teaspoon ground coriander
2 teaspoons ground cumin
2 eggs
1/4 teaspoon ground white pepper
1/2 cup (90 g) rice flour
1/2 cup (60 g) plain flour
peanut oil, for shallow-frying

Sauce
1/3 cup (80 ml) lime juice
2 tablespoons tamarind concentrate (see Note)
2 tablespoons grated palm sugar or soft brown sugar
2 tablespoons fish sauce
1 clove garlic, crushed

1 Put the prawns, sweet potato, spring onion, garlic, ginger, fresh and ground coriander, cumin, eggs, pepper and 1 teaspoon salt in a large bowl and mix well. Stir in the flours until combined—the mixture will be sticky.

2 Combine the sauce ingredients in a bowl. Stir until the sugar dissolves.

3 Heat a little of the oil in a large frying pan over medium heat. Drop tablespoons of the batter into the oil, flattening with the back of a lightly oiled spatula. Cook for 1–2 minutes on each side or until crisp and golden. Drain on paper towels and keep warm. Repeat with the remaining oil and batter. Serve hot with a drizzling of sauce.

Nutrition per fritter: Fat 3 g; Protein 5.5 g; Carbohydrate 7.5 g; Dietary Fibre 0.5 g; Cholesterol 46 mg; 330 kJ (80 Cal)

Note: Make sure you don't buy tamarind purée by mistake.

Prawn, ricotta and spinach pasta (top), and Prawn and sweet potato fritters

TOM YUM GOONG
(Hot and sour
prawn soup)
Prep time: 20 minutes
Cooking time: 40 minutes
Serves 4

1 kg raw medium prawns
1 tablespoon oil
2 tablespoons tom yum
  paste
2 stems lemon grass (white
  part only), bruised
4 fresh kaffir lime leaves
3 small fresh red chillies,
  thinly sliced
80–100 ml fish sauce
80–100 ml lime juice
2 teaspoons grated palm
  sugar or soft brown sugar
4 spring onions, thinly sliced
  on the diagonal
4 tablespoons fresh
  coriander leaves

1 Peel and devein the
prawns, leaving the tails
intact. Reserve the shells
and heads. Cover the
prawns and refrigerate.
2 Heat a wok over high
heat, add the oil and
swirl to coat. Cook the
prawn shells and heads
over medium heat for
8–10 minutes, or until
they turn orange.
3 Add the tom yum
paste and 1/4 cup (60 ml)
water and cook for
1 minute, or until
fragrant. Add 2.2 litres
water, bring to the boil,
then reduce the heat and
simmer for 20 minutes.
Strain into a large bowl,

discarding the shells and
heads, and return the
stock to the wok.
4 Add the prawns, lemon
grass, lime leaves and
chilli and simmer for
4–5 minutes, or until the
prawns are cooked. Stir
in the fish sauce, lime
juice, sugar, spring onion
and coriander. Discard
the lemon grass and
serve immediately.

Nutrition per serve: Fat 9 g;
Protein 29 g; Carbohydrate 4.5 g;
Dietary Fibre 2 g; Cholesterol
186.5 mg; 905 kJ (215 Cal)

PRAWN
POTSTICKERS
Prep time: 25 minutes
Cooking time: 10 minutes
Makes 24

Dipping sauce
1/4 cup (60 ml) soy sauce
1 spring onion, thinly sliced
1 clove garlic, crushed
1/4 teaspoon finely chopped
  fresh ginger
1/4 teaspoon sesame oil

500 g raw medium prawns
40 g Chinese cabbage, finely
  shredded
40 g drained water
  chestnuts, finely chopped
1 tablespoon finely chopped
  fresh coriander leaves
24 round gow gee wrappers
  (see Note)
1 tablespoon vegetable oil
1/2 cup (125 ml) chicken
  stock

1 To make the dipping
sauce, mix together all
the ingredients in a
small bowl.
2 Peel and devein the
prawns, then finely chop.
Combine the prawn
meat, cabbage, water
chestnuts and coriander.
3 Lay all the gow gee
wrappers out on a work
surface and put one
heaped teaspoon of the
prawn filling in the
centre of each. Moisten
the edges with water and
draw together into the
shape of a moneybag,
pressing the edges
together firmly to seal.
4 Heat the oil in a large
frying pan and add the
potstickers. Cook in
batches over medium
heat for 2 minutes, or
until just brown on the
bottom. Add the stock,
then quickly cover with
a lid as it will spit. Steam
for 2–3 minutes, taking
care that all the stock
does not evaporate and
the potstickers do not
burn. Serve immediately
with the dipping sauce.

Nutrition per potsticker: Fat 1 g;
Protein 3 g; Carbohydrate 5 g;
Dietary Fibre 0.5 g; Cholesterol
16 mg; 170 kJ (40 Cal)

Note: Gow gee wrappers are
rolled out round pieces of dough
made from wheat flour and
water. They are available from
Asian food stores.

Tom yum goong (top), and
Prawn potstickers

PRAWN RAVIOLI WITH KAFFIR LIME SAUCE

Prep time: 30 minutes
Cooking time: 10 minutes
Serves 4

700 g raw medium prawns
2 spring onions, thinly sliced
1 tablespoon chopped fresh coriander
1 tablespoon fish sauce
2 teaspoons finely chopped fresh ginger
ground white pepper, to taste
48 gow gee wrappers (see Notes)
1 egg, lightly beaten
1 teaspoon oil
fresh kaffir lime leaves, shredded, to garnish

Kaffir lime sauce
30 g butter
2 spring onions, thinly sliced
2 cloves garlic, crushed
5–6 large fresh kaffir lime leaves, thinly shredded
300 ml cream
1/3 cup (80 ml) chicken stock
1 1/2 teaspoons lime or lemon juice
1 tablespoon fish sauce

1 Peel and devein the prawns. Blend 350 g of the prawns in a food processor until well minced, then transfer to a bowl. Slice the remaining prawns into 1 cm pieces and add to the bowl with the minced prawns. Add the spring onion, coriander, fish sauce, ginger and white pepper and mix together well.

2 To assemble the ravioli, place 24 gow gee wrappers on a board. Place about 1 heaped teaspoon of the prawn filling into the middle of each wrapper. Brush the edges lightly with the beaten egg and lay the remaining wrappers over the top to enclose the filling. Press the edges together to seal. Cover with a damp tea towel and place in the fridge until required.

3 To make the sauce, melt the butter in a small saucepan over medium–low heat and add the spring onion, garlic and kaffir lime leaves. Stir gently for about 1 minute, or until aromatic. Be careful that the garlic doesn't burn or the sauce will taste bitter. Add the cream and stock and simmer for 3–4 minutes or until slightly reduced, then add the lime juice and fish sauce. Season to taste with salt and cracked black pepper.

4 Meanwhile, to cook the ravioli, fill a deep frying pan with 4–5 cm of water and add the oil. Bring the water to the boil and cook the ravioli in batches for about 2–3 minutes, or until the filling is cooked and the gow gee wrappers are soft. Scoop out the ravioli with a slotted spoon and place six pieces on each plate.

5 To serve, spoon the hot sauce over the ravioli and garnish with extra shredded kaffir lime leaves.

Nutrition per serve: Fat 43 g; Protein 32 g; Carbohydrate 59 g; Dietary Fibre 2.5 g; Cholesterol 305 mg; 3135 kJ (750 Cal)

Notes: Gow gee wrappers are round pieces of dough made from wheat flour and water. You will need about 1 1/2 packets to get 48 wrappers. They are available at Asian food stores and some supermarkets.

Kaffir lime leaves are available fresh or dried. The fragrant leaves are shaped in a figure of eight, but they are often broken up by the time they reach the greengrocer. In our recipes, one half of the figure of eight represents one leaf.

Prawn ravioli with kaffir lime sauce

PRAWN AND SNOW PEA STIR-FRY

Prep time: 25 minutes
Cooking time: 10 minutes
Serves 4–6

1 1/2 tablespoons peanut oil
3 cloves garlic, thinly sliced
1 stem lemon grass (white part only), finely chopped
1 1/2 tablespoons thinly sliced fresh ginger
1 kg raw medium prawns, peeled and deveined, with tails intact
200 g snow peas, trimmed and cut into 3–4 strips lengthways
6 spring onions, cut into thin slices on the diagonal
75 g snow pea sprouts
1 tablespoon Chinese rice wine or dry sherry
1 tablespoon oyster sauce
1 tablespoon soy sauce

1 Heat a wok to very hot, add the oil and swirl to coat the side. Add the garlic, lemon grass and ginger and stir-fry for 1–2 minutes, or until fragrant. Add the prawns and cook for 2–3 minutes, or until pink and cooked.
2 Add the snow peas, spring onion, sprouts, rice wine, oyster and soy sauces and toss until heated through and the vegetables start to wilt.

Nutrition per serve (6): Fat 1.5 g; Protein 19.5 g; Carbohydrate 6 g; Dietary Fibre 2 g; Cholesterol 124 mg; 515 kJ (125 Cal)

TEMPURA PRAWNS ON SOBA NOODLES

Prep time: 25 minutes
Cooking time: 15 minutes
Serves 4

12 raw large prawns
1 sachet (10 g) instant dashi granules
1/4 cup (60 ml) Japanese soy sauce
2 tablespoons mirin
150 g soba noodles
oil, for deep-frying
1 egg
1 cup (250 ml) iced water
1 cup (125 g) tempura flour, sifted
2 ice cubes
1 sheet roasted nori, shredded

1 Peel and devein the prawns, leaving the tails intact. Make three or four shallow incisions into the underside of each prawn, then dry them with paper towel.
2 Dissolve the dashi in 1 litre boiling water in a saucepan. Stir in the soy sauce and mirin, cover and keep warm.
3 Bring a saucepan of water to the boil and gradually add the noodles, stirring to stop them from sticking. Return the water to the boil and, when it starts to foam, pour in 1 cup (250 ml) of cold water. Do this 2–3 times and cook for about 4–5 minutes in total.

Taste to check that they are tender, then drain, rinse under hot water and keep warm.
4 Fill a wok or large saucepan one third full of oil and heat to 180°C (350°F), or until a cube of bread dropped in the oil browns in 15 seconds. To make the batter, place the egg in a large bowl and beat lightly with chopsticks or a fork. Mix in the iced water with chopsticks. Add the flour all at once and mix until just combined—the mixture should be lumpy. Add the ice.
5 Dip four prawns in the batter, then deep-fry for 1 minute, or until crisp and lightly golden. Drain on crumpled paper towels and keep warm. Repeat with the remaining prawns.
6 Gently reheat the broth if necessary over medium heat until hot. To serve, divide the noodles among four deep serving bowls and cover with the hot broth. Arrange the prawns on the top, garnish with the nori and serve immediately.

Nutrition per serve: Fat 17.5 g; Protein 21 g; Carbohydrate 44 g; Dietary Fibre 4.5 g; Cholesterol 134 mg; 1795 kJ (430 Cal)

Prawn and snow pea stir-fry (top), and Tempura prawns on soba noodles

...WN AND ...NNEL SALAD

...rep time: 20 minutes
Cooking time: 5 minutes
Serves 4 (entrée)

750 g raw large prawns,
  peeled and deveined
1 fennel bulb, thinly sliced
  (400 g)
200 g watercress
1 1/2 tablespoons finely
  chopped fresh chives
1/3 cup (80 ml) extra virgin
  olive oil
2 tablespoons lemon juice
2 teaspoons Dijon mustard
1 clove garlic, finely
  chopped

1 Bring a saucepan of water to the boil, then add the prawns, return to the boil and simmer for 2 minutes, or until the prawns turn pink and are cooked through. Drain and leave to cool. Pat the prawns dry with paper towels and slice in half lengthways. Place in a large serving bowl.
2 Add the fennel, watercress and chives to the bowl and mix well.
3 To make the dressing, whisk the oil, lemon juice, mustard and garlic together in a small bowl until combined. Pour the dressing over the salad, season with salt

Prawn and fennel salad
(top), and Prawn pâté
with garlic toasts

and cracked black pepper and toss gently. Arrange the salad on individual serving plates and serve immediately.

Nutrition per serve: Fat 18 g;
Protein 22 g; Carbohydrate 4 g;
Dietary Fibre 5 g; Cholesterol
139.5 mg; 1115 kJ (265 Cal)

PRAWN PATE WITH GARLIC TOASTS

Prep time: 25 minutes +
  2 hours refrigeration +
  50 minutes standing
Cooking time: 10 minutes
Serves 8

1 1/4 cups (315 ml) chicken
  stock
1 tablespoon gelatine
375 g cream cheese, at
  room temperature
800 g cooked prawns,
  peeled and deveined
2 cloves garlic, crushed
2 tablespoons finely
  chopped fresh chives
1 tablespoon chopped
  fresh dill
30 g butter, melted
2 tablespoons olive oil
1 French bread stick, cut
  into 7 mm slices

1 Bring a shallow saucepan of water to the boil. Pour the stock into a heatproof bowl, then sprinkle the gelatine evenly onto it; do not stir. Remove the saucepan from the heat and place the bowl of

chicken stock in the pan. Stir the gelatine into the stock until it has dissolved; remove the bowl and leave to cool for 30 minutes.
2 Place the gelatine liquid in a blender, add the cream cheese, half the prawn meat and half of the garlic and blend until smooth. Transfer to a bowl and leave for 20 minutes, or until thickened slightly.
3 Add the remaining prawn meat, chives and dill and season to taste. Pour into eight 1/2 cup (125 ml) ramekins. Cover with plastic wrap and refrigerate for 2 hours, or until set.
4 Preheat the oven to moderate 180°C (350°F/Gas 4). Combine the butter, oil and remaining garlic and lightly brush both sides of the bread slices with the mixture. Place apart on baking trays and bake for 10 minutes, or until golden and crisp. Leave to cool.
5 Unmould the pâté and serve with the garlic toasts.

Nutrition per serve: Fat 24 g;
Protein 19 g; Carbohydrate 12 g;
Dietary Fibre 1 g; Cholesterol
148.5 mg; 1390 kJ (330 Cal)

Index